Leadersl

by Kelly Gaffney

A leader is someone who helps people
to do the right thing.
People will listen to a leader.
They will often do things
that a leader asks them to do.

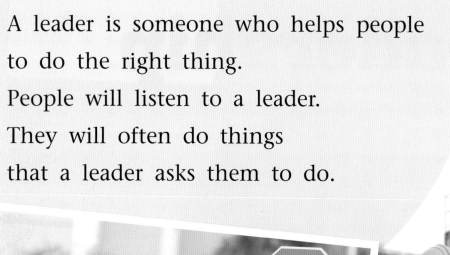

Anyone can be a leader.
A good leader is someone
who people look up to.

There are leaders at your school.
The head *teacher* is a leader.
The teachers and children at your school
listen to the head teacher.

Your teacher is
a leader, too.
The children
in your class listen
to the teacher.

You might think you have to wait
until you grow up to be a leader.
But you don't.
Children can be leaders, too.

5

Look around your school, and you will see
lots of children who are leaders.

Some children are leaders
because they show others
the right way to act.
These children help
when they see things
that need to be done.
They may have special jobs
or help young children.

If you would like to be a leader,
there are things you need to know.

A good leader is *brave*.
You might think that it is easy to be brave,
but it can be very hard.
Brave children follow the rules
even if their friends do not.

It's also brave to tell
children to stop,
if they are being
mean to someone.

9

Good leaders always try to do their best.
When you try something new,
it can take a long time to do it well.
Keep trying, and never give up.
Don't worry about making a *mistake*
because everybody makes mistakes.

To be a good leader,
you must work
as part of a team.

Talk nicely to people around you,
and ask them to talk nicely to each other.
You need to listen to what other people have to say.
You shouldn't be bossy.

Good leaders are kind,
and they help other people.

You can show
you are a good leader
by working well
with other children.

Good leaders play nicely outside, too.
If you see someone has been left out,
go and ask them to play.

13

A good leader helps young children at school.

You can help if a young child gets hurt
and needs to find a teacher.

Sometimes you can even help
young children think of a game to play.

Would you like to be a leader?

Think about the things
that you can do to help other people.

Picture glossary

brave

teacher

young

mistake

team